This book is dedicated to everyone who believed in me and showed me unconditional love.

AF616736

Layla's Story

Varanda Vallisto

Layla's Story
Copyright © 2023 Varanda Vallisto

All rights reserved. No portion of this book may be reproduced in any form without written permission from the publisher.

To request permission, contact **Varandavallistobooks@gmail.com**

ISBN: 979-8-218-21674-0

Printed In the United States of America

First printing, 2023.

It was cold and snowy on the night Layla was born. Layla grew to have bright, sparkling blue eyes and a smile always on her face.

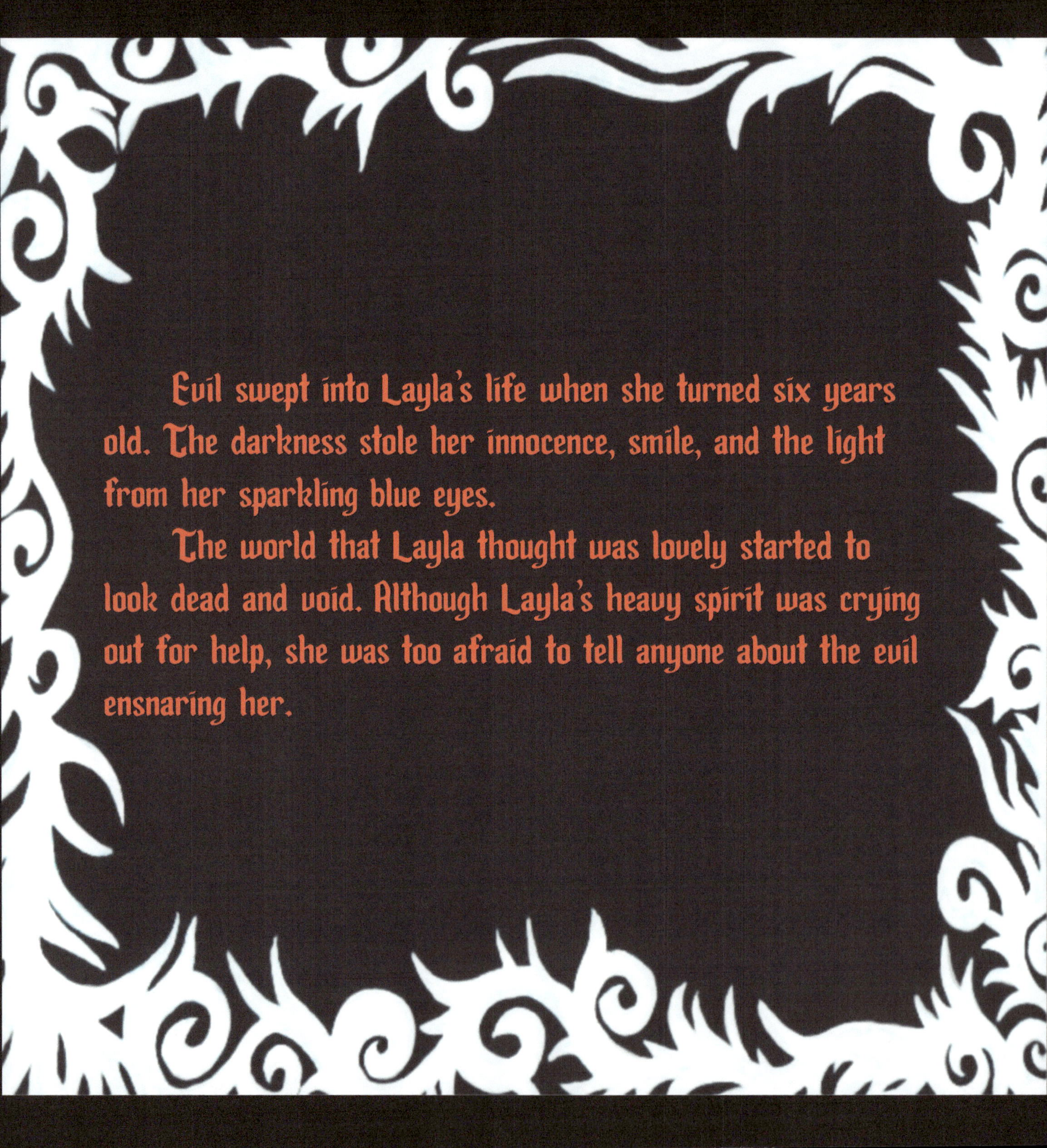

Evil swept into Layla's life when she turned six years old. The darkness stole her innocence, smile, and the light from her sparkling blue eyes.

The world that Layla thought was lovely started to look dead and void. Although Layla's heavy spirit was crying out for help, she was too afraid to tell anyone about the evil ensnaring her.

473
x180

623
x400

Jan 1, 2004

328
x200

F-

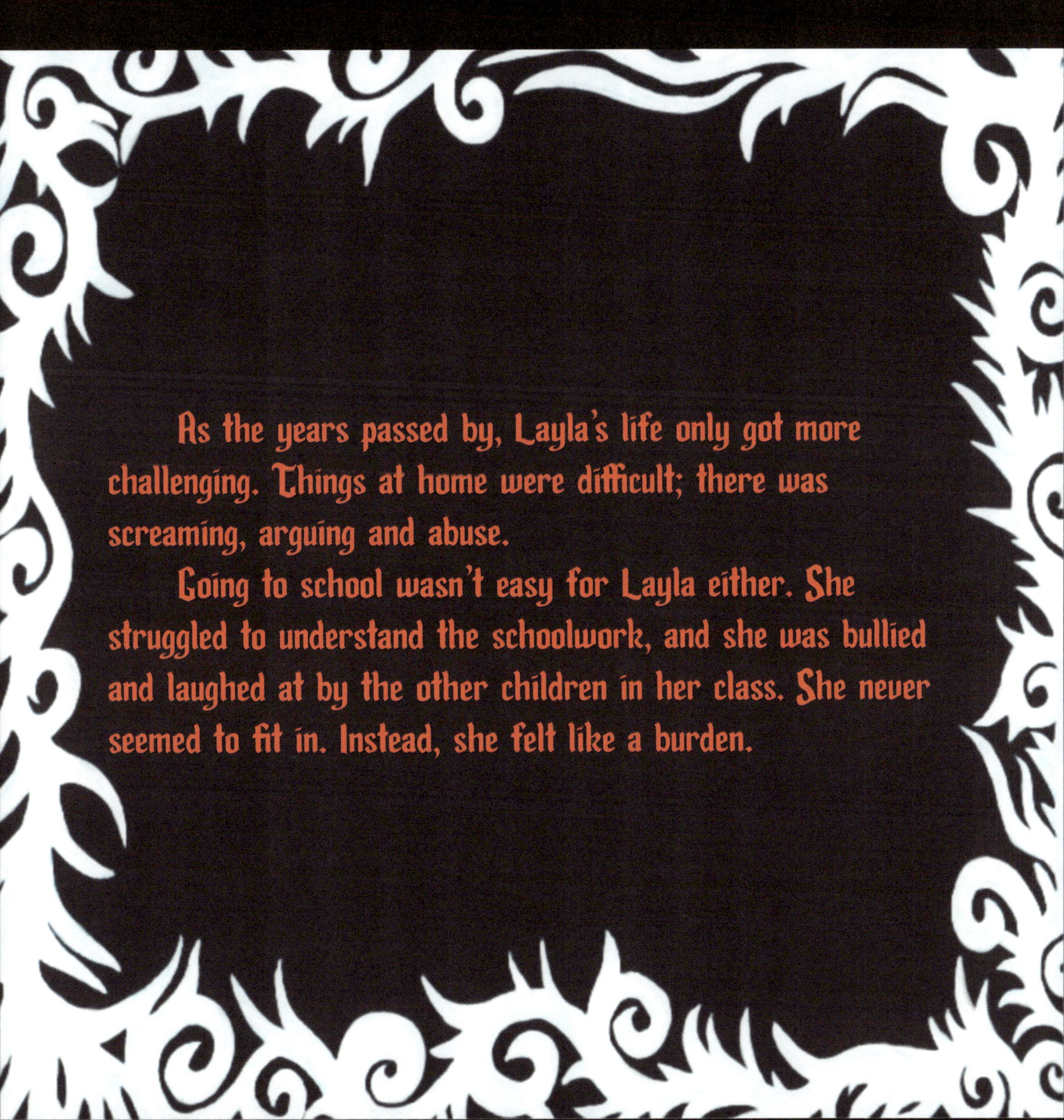

As the years passed by, Layla's life only got more challenging. Things at home were difficult; there was screaming, arguing and abuse.

Going to school wasn't easy for Layla either. She struggled to understand the schoolwork, and she was bullied and laughed at by the other children in her class. She never seemed to fit in. Instead, she felt like a burden.

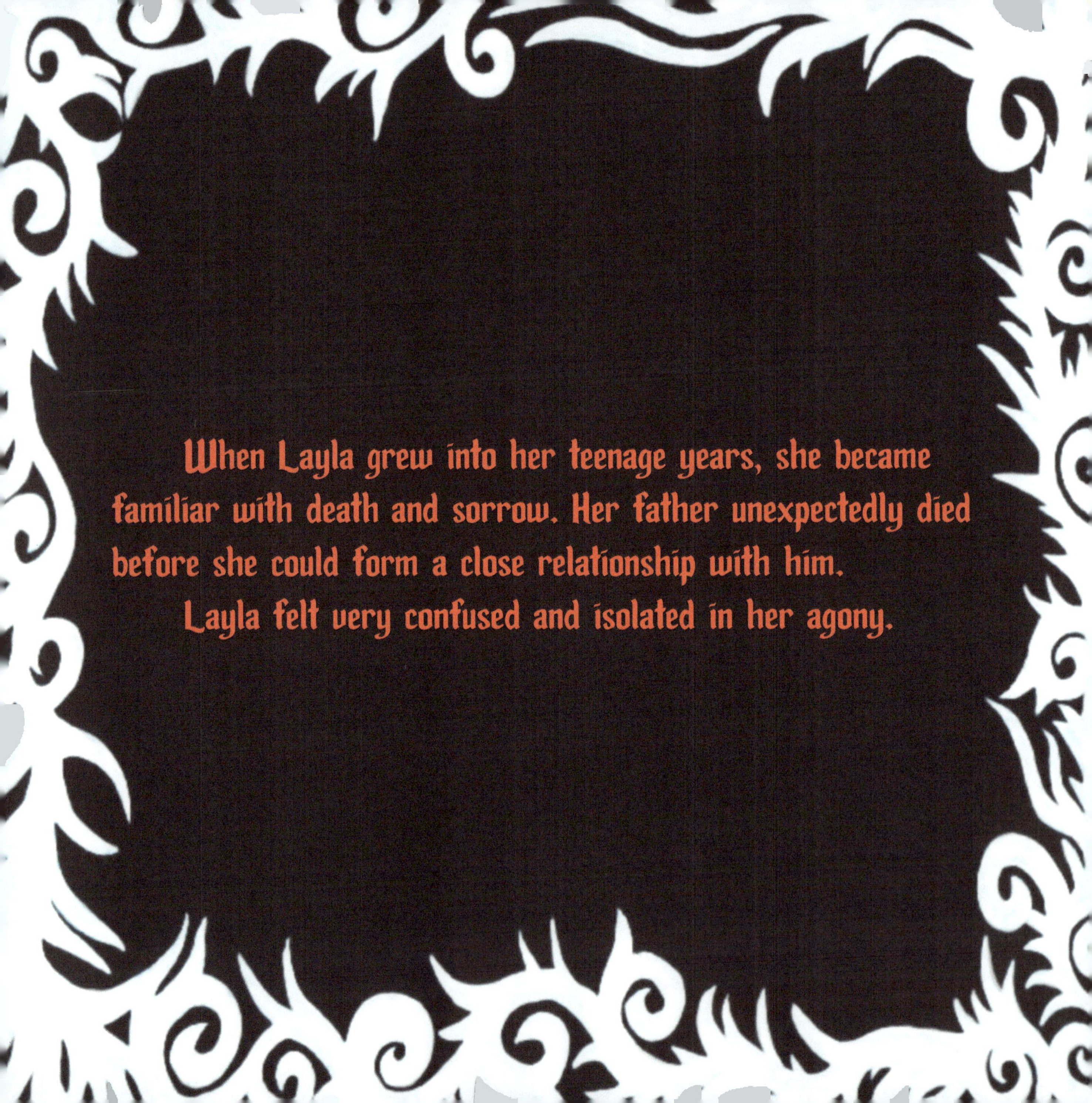

When Layla grew into her teenage years, she became familiar with death and sorrow. Her father unexpectedly died before she could form a close relationship with him.

Layla felt very confused and isolated in her agony.

RIP

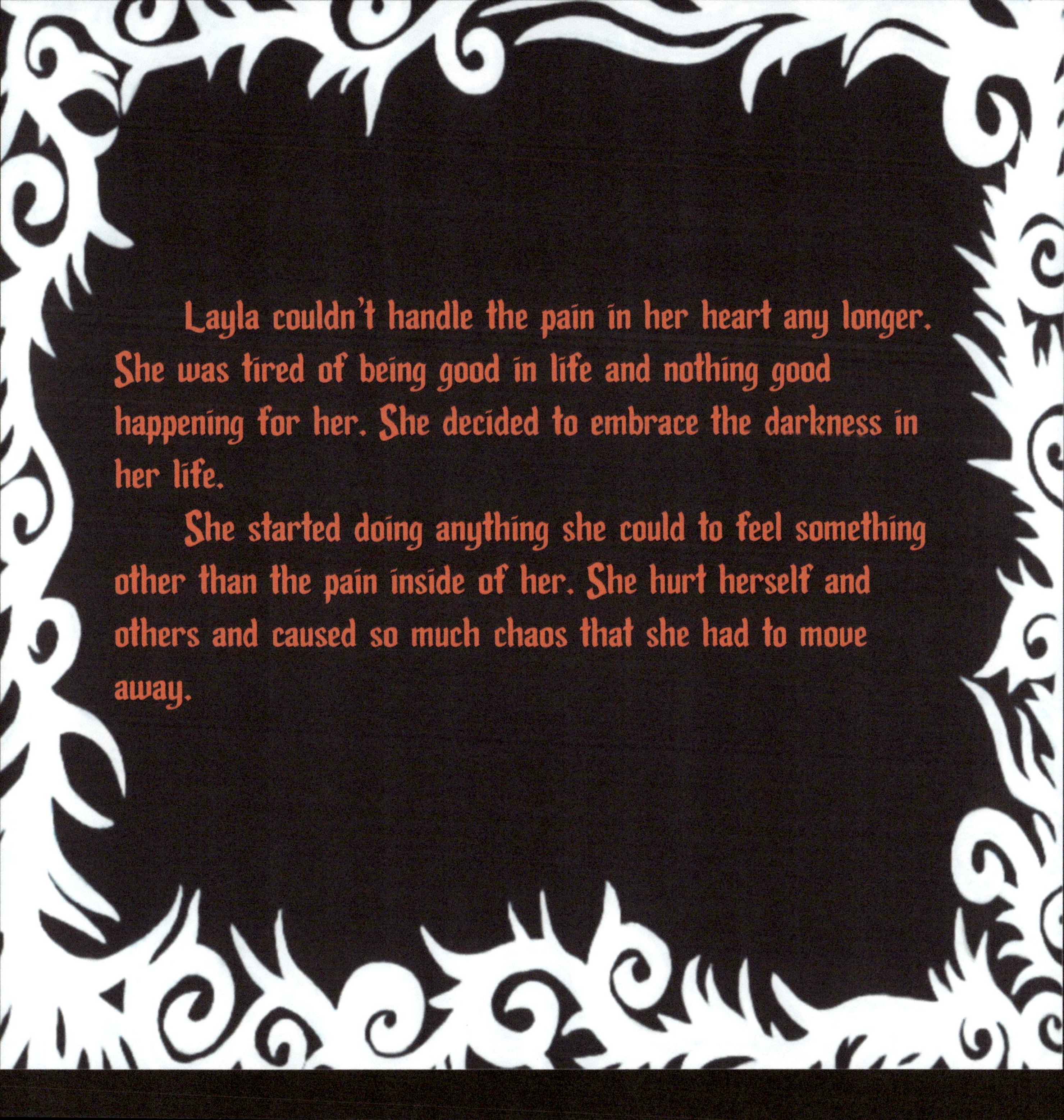

Layla couldn't handle the pain in her heart any longer. She was tired of being good in life and nothing good happening for her. She decided to embrace the darkness in her life.

She started doing anything she could to feel something other than the pain inside of her. She hurt herself and others and caused so much chaos that she had to move away.

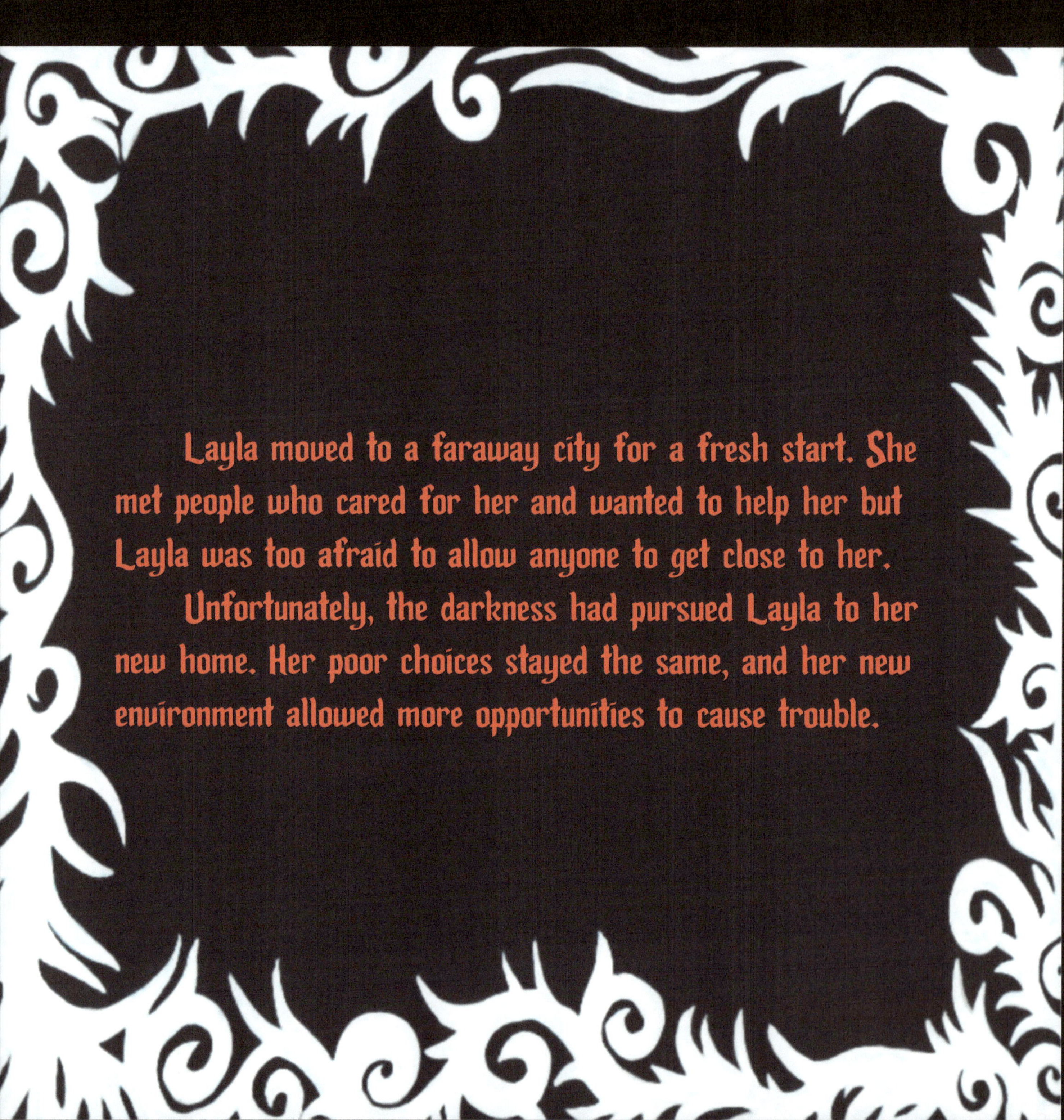

Layla moved to a faraway city for a fresh start. She met people who cared for her and wanted to help her but Layla was too afraid to allow anyone to get close to her.

Unfortunately, the darkness had pursued Layla to her new home. Her poor choices stayed the same, and her new environment allowed more opportunities to cause trouble.

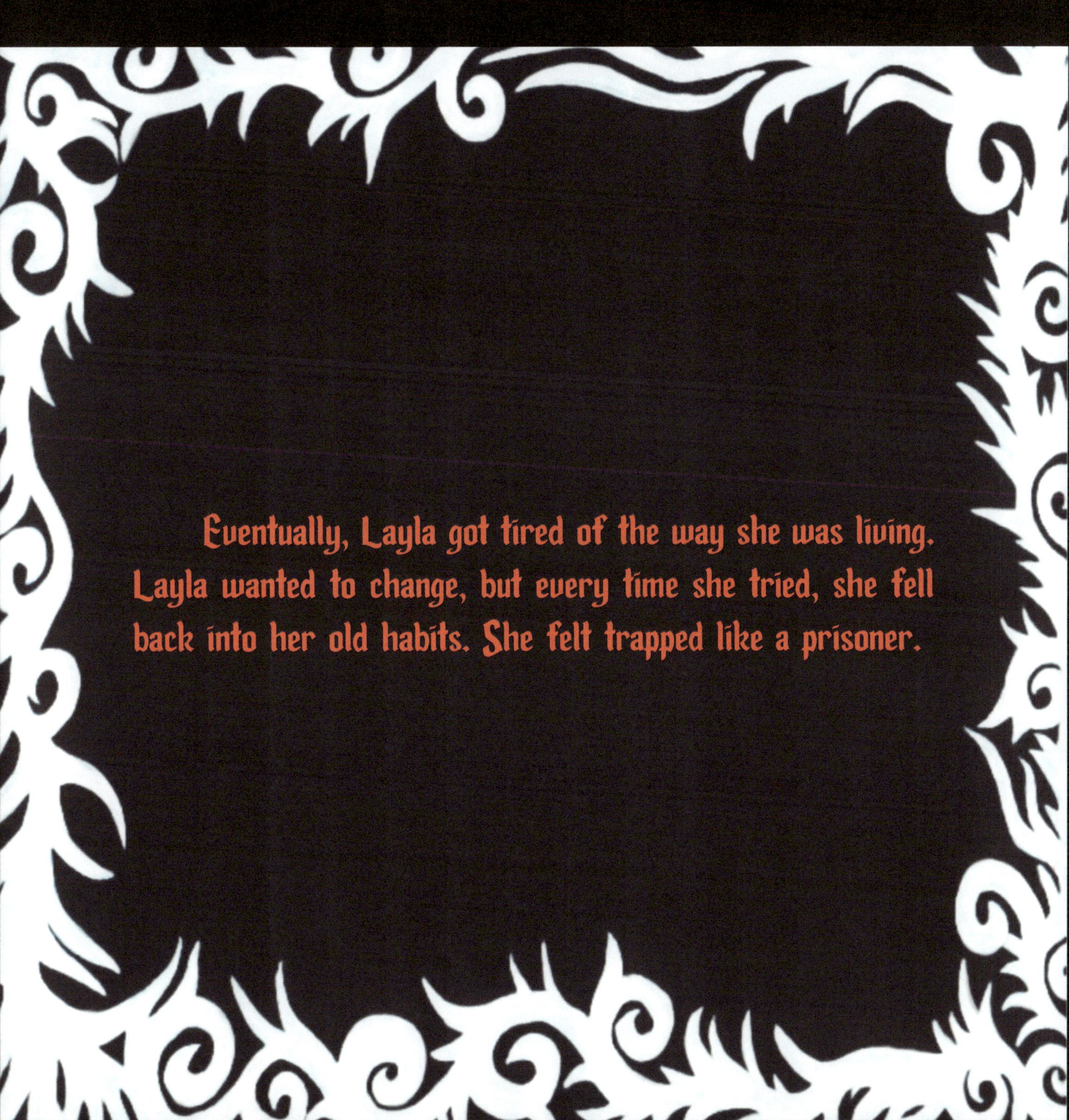

Eventually, Layla got tired of the way she was living. Layla wanted to change, but every time she tried, she fell back into her old habits. She felt trapped like a prisoner.

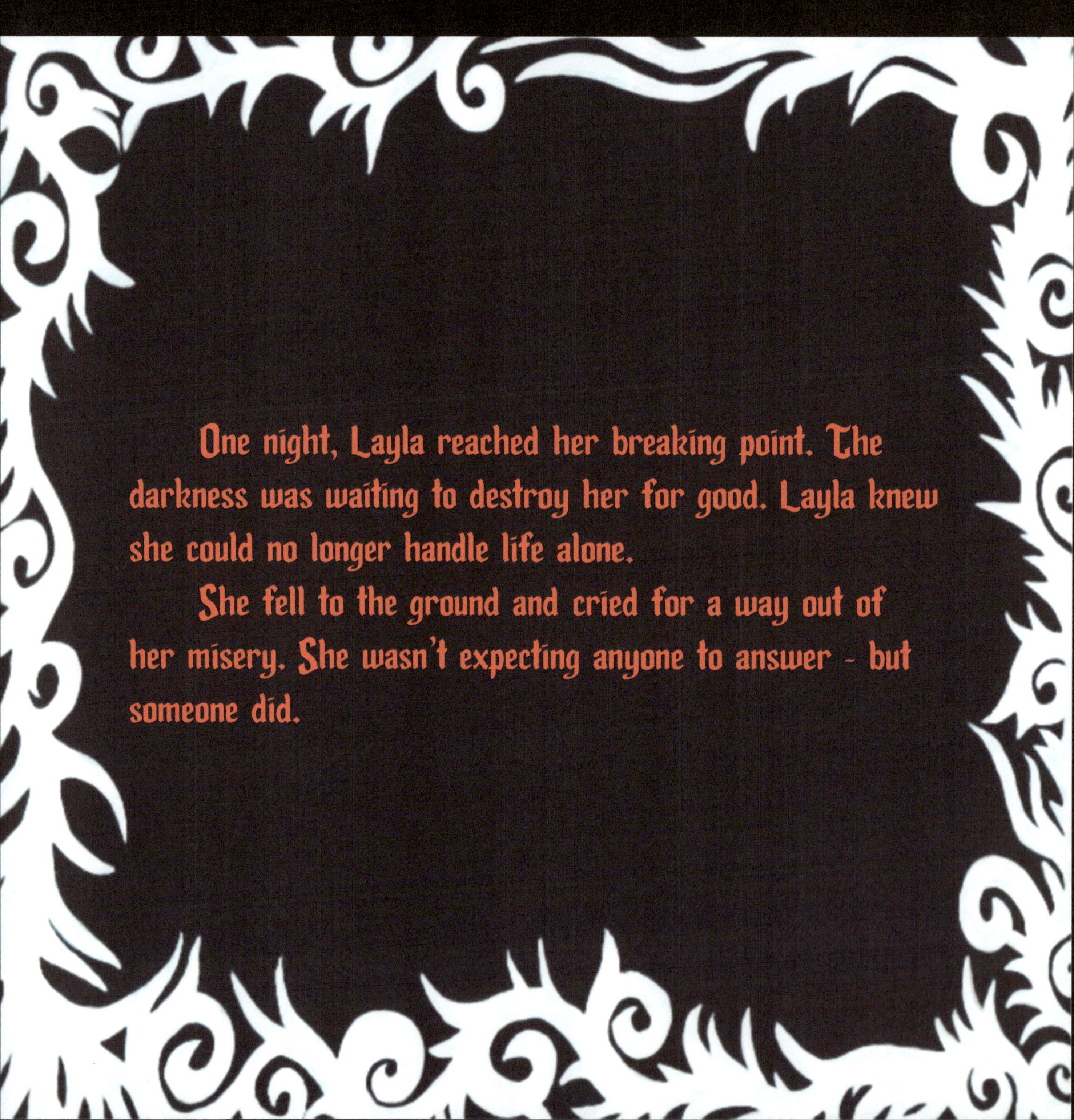

One night, Layla reached her breaking point. The darkness was waiting to destroy her for good. Layla knew she could no longer handle life alone.

She fell to the ground and cried for a way out of her misery. She wasn't expecting anyone to answer - but someone did.

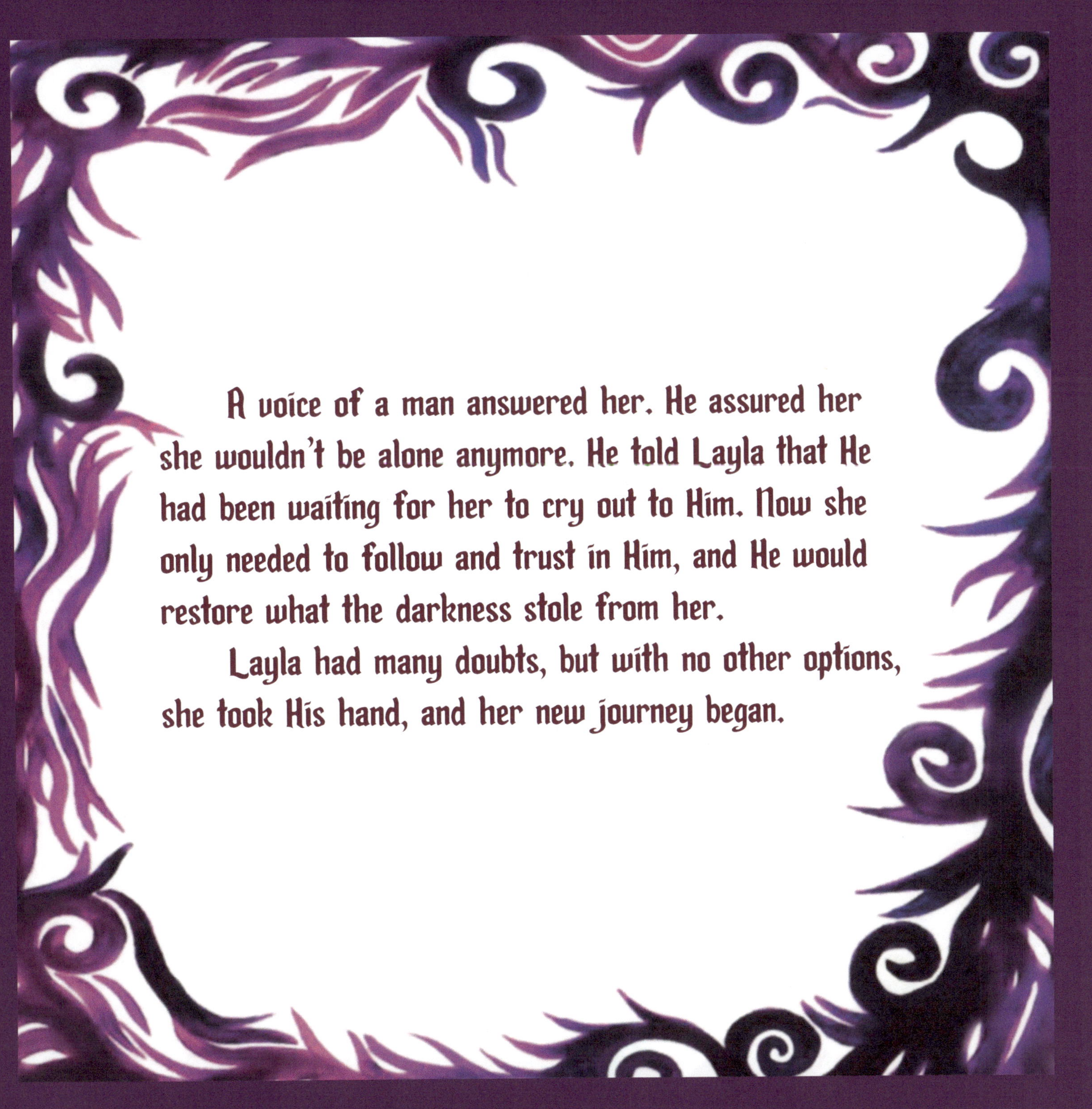

A voice of a man answered her. He assured her she wouldn't be alone anymore. He told Layla that He had been waiting for her to cry out to Him. Now she only needed to follow and trust in Him, and He would restore what the darkness stole from her.

Layla had many doubts, but with no other options, she took His hand, and her new journey began.

Day by day, Layla was transformed into a new creation. She made amends with the people she hurt and began to heal from her past. Her new life was not always easy, but even during the hard times and dark days, Layla could see life's beauty again.

Layla was free and felt true peace. Her smile and the light in her sparkling blue eyes had finally returned.

The End

Author's Note

Layla's Story is based on events that took place throughout my life. My earliest childhood memories remind me that I am a survivor of sexual, physical, and emotional abuse.

When I reached my teenage years, I had no idea how to cope with these hidden afflictions. To self-soothe, I began harming myself with drugs, suicide attempts, and criminal activity. I tried anything I could to escape the pain I felt inside, even though the relief was only temporary.

My attempts to self-medicate quickly led me down a path of self-destruction. At just fifteen years old, my actions landed me in a juvenile detention center. Living in jail wasn't what I wanted for my life, but I had unresolved pain within me that kept me trapped in a toxic cycle.

Eventually, I reached my breaking point—where Jesus met me and offered me a new beginning. I learned that Jesus was not a temporary fix like my other vices, but a forever solution to all my past and future pain. Since making the decision to follow Him, the Lord has renewed my life and given me a new identity and a purpose here on earth. Praise God!

"Therefore, if any man be in Christ, he is a new creature: old things are passed away; behold, all things become new."

— 2 Corinthians 5:17

Follow my artwork on Instagram:

@secretplacestudio

www.ingramcontent.com/pod-product-compliance
Ingram Content Group UK Ltd.
Pitfield, Milton Keynes, MK11 3LW, UK
UKHW061500070726
13610UKWH00005B/8
9798218216740